MY
Beautiful
NIGERIA

Things I know about the Giant of Africa

Eke Amba

ISBN: 1-4392-0720-8
ISBN-13: 9781439207208

Visit www.Amazon.com to order additional copies or
e-mail ekeamba@hotmail.com

For those who want to learn simple
facts about Nigeria: her rich history, her diverse cultures,
her governments and her people

Inside

The Country at a Glance

The Name and Location

The official name of Nigeria is "The Federal Republic of Nigeria." The name "Nigeria" was first suggested by Flora Shaw in 1897. At the time, Flora Shaw was an editor with The Times newspaper. Flora Shaw later married Lord Frederick Luggard. Lord Luggard was the first Governor General of Nigeria.

The name "Nigeria" is a combination of the words "Niger" and "area." Niger refers to the River Niger. Nigeria was created through the amalgamation (the joining) of the areas around the north and south of the River Niger into one country.

Nigeria is located in the Gulf of Guinea, in West Africa. To the west of Nigeria is the Republic of Benin. To the north of Nigeria is the Republic of Niger. To the south of Nigeria is the Gulf of Guinea on the Atlantic Ocean. To the east of Nigeria are Cameroon and Chad.

Map of Nigeria

This map shows the River Niger and the River Benue (the largest rivers in Nigeria). The River Niger flows from the northwestern part of Nigeria down toward the southeast, and forms a "Y" confluence with another river, the River Benue, and from there flows into the Atlantic Ocean. The map also shows the countries that surround Nigeria.

Coat of Arms: National Symbol

The Coat of Arms is a symbol that represents Nigeria. Every aspect of the Coat of Arms represents something about the country.

The black shield stands for Nigeria's earth or land. The silver wavy bends in the middle of the black shield represent the River Niger and the River Benue, and their confluence.

The country is split into three parts by the two biggest rivers that run through Nigeria; the River Niger and the River Benue. The River Niger is the third longest river in Africa.

The flowers on which the shield stands are Costus Spectabilis (the national flower). The wreath above the shield features the national colors: green and white. The eagle represents strength. The horses stand for dignity. The words "Unity and Faith, Peace and Progress" are the country's motto.

States and Resources

Nigeria is currently divided into thirty-six states, in addition to the Federal Capital Territory, Abuja. Nigeria has many natural resources, the most important of which is crude oil (or petroleum). Nigeria is one of the world's largest producers of crude oil. Other important natural resources in Nigeria are limestone, coal, lead, zinc, iron, tin and niobium.

Nigeria produces various agricultural products, such as cassava, millet, timber, rubber, cocoa, palm oil and ground-nuts (or peanuts). Nigeria is also the source of many non-agricultural products, including cement, other construction materials, footwear, chemicals, fertilizer, ceramics and steel.

Climate and Seasons

The climate in Nigeria varies from region to region. Nigeria can be divided into three climatic regions: the far north, the far south and the areas in between.

The far north, which is close to the Sahara Desert, is characterized by desert-like climate, with extreme weather conditions.
Temperatures are generally very high during the day and very low, close to freezing at night. For example, Kano state is located in the far north of the country and temperatures in Kano can reach a high of 38°C (100.4°F) and drop as low as 14°C (57.2°F).

The far south, which is close to the Atlantic Ocean, is characterized by tropical rain forest climate and experiences lots of rain and generally lower temperatures for most of the year. For example, Lagos state is located in the far southwest of the country and temperatures in Lagos vary between a low of 22°C (71.6°F) and a high of 33°C (91.4°F).

The areas in between the far north and the far south have somewhat milder temperatures (not too high and not too low) throughout the year.

The seasons, just like the climate, vary from region to region. In general, Nigeria has two major seasons, known as the dry (or harmattan) season and the wet (or rainy) season.

In the far north, the dry season begins in October and ends in April. In the far south, the dry season begins in November and ends in March. In the areas in between the far north and the far south, the dry season begins at varying times but does not start as early as it does in the far north. The wet season lasts for the remainder of the year. During the wet season, there is a lot of rain and temperatures are cooler. During the dry season, there is very little rain and the temperatures are generally very high.

The Flag

The colors of the Nigerian flag are green and white. Green stands for agriculture, and white stands for peace. The flag was chosen through a contest that featured almost 3000 entries. M.T.S. Akinkunmi had the winning entry. Akinkunmi was completing his post-graduate studies in Agricultural Engineering at the time of the competition. His winning entry had the symbol of the sun in the middle, but it was removed when his entry was chosen. It became the official flag of Nigeria on Independence Day, October 1, 1960.

Abuja – The Federal Capital Territory

People relaxing at the Millennium Park in Abuja, Nigeria.

Abuja is the Federal Capital Territory or the capital city of Nigeria. The presidential house, also called Aso Rock, and other major governmental offices are located in Abuja.

Until December 21, 1991, Lagos was the capital city of Nigeria. Lagos is located in the western part of Nigeria, and Abuja is centered in the middle of the country. As such, it was concluded that Abuja was a more appropriate location for the capital city.

Lagos is considered the economic center of Nigeria because many businesses are located in Lagos.
Other major commercial cities are Onitsha, Kano, Ibadan, Port Harcourt, Aba, Maiduguri, Jos, Kaduna, Warri, Benin and Nnewi.

The People of Nigeria

Nigeria is the most populous country on the continent of Africa. About every one in four Africans is a Nigerian. There are more than 135 million people and over 250 ethnic groups in Nigeria. The official language in Nigeria is English, and many Nigerians speak more than one of the approximately 250 indigenous languages.

The most populous ethnic groups in Nigeria are the Hausas, the Igbos and the Yorubas. Other smaller but populous ethnic groups in Nigeria are the Fulanis, the Ijaws, the Kanuris, the Ibibios and the Tivs.

The Hausas

Hausa is mainly spoken in the northern part of Nigeria, in Kano, Kaduna, Bauchi, Sokoto, Katsina, Kebbi and Zamfara.

The independent Hausa cities were united by the Jihad (holy war) led by Usman Dan Fodio in the 19th century. The traditional occupation of the Hausas is farming. The Hausas are also known for their leatherwork, embroidery and dyeing materials.

Traditional Hausa food crops include corn, sorghum, rice and millet. A popular Hausa meal is tuwo (rice porridge).

Hausa Proverbs:

Even the River Niger must flow around an island.

If you do not like the phases of the moon, get a ladder and repair it.

A man in modern traditional Hausa dressing: a long flowing robe embroidered in the middle (called babban riga) worn over a kaftan and a pair of pants (trousers) with a cap to match. A woman in modern traditional Hausa dressing: a blouse and wrapper with a matching head scarf. Sometimes, as shown here, a shawl is draped around the shoulders. The shawl is sometimes wrapped around the head and draped over the shoulders.

The Igbos

Igbo is mainly spoken in the southeastern part of the country, in Abia, Anambra, Ebonyi, Enugu and Imo states. Igbo is also spoken in parts of Delta and Rivers states.

Historically, the Igbos lived in separate, local societies and villages, and they were not governed by a single governing body. The traditional occupation of the Igbos is farming and the Igbos are also known for their carved masks that are used as part of traditional ceremonies.

Traditional Igbo food crops include yams, cassava, cocoyams and plantains. A popular Igbo meal is Isi-Ewu (goat head pepper soup).

Igbo Proverbs:

A man who believes he can do everything should dig a grave and bury himself.

When a handshake goes beyond the elbow, it has become something else.

A woman dressed in modern traditional Igbo dressing, which consists of a beautiful blouse, two wrappers (one long, one short) and a matching head gear.

The Yorubas

Yoruba is mainly spoken in the southwestern part of Nigeria, in Ekiti, Oyo, Osun, Ogun, Ondo, Kwara, Lagos and Kogi states.

According to Yoruba mythology, the world began in one of the Yoruba cities, named Ile-Ife; Ile-Ife is said to be the center of the universe. The Yorubas are known for their life-sized bronze heads, terracotta, weaving, dyeing and metal work.

Traditional Yoruba food crops include corn, cassavas and yams. Popular Yoruba meals are eko (corn pudding) and amala (yam flour made into a paste-like consistency) eaten with a soup made with chopped vegetable leaves and/or Okra.

Yoruba Proverbs:

The river that forgets its source will dry up.

Words are like eggs; once they are spoken, they can't be taken back.

A couple dressed in modern traditional Yoruba clothes on their wedding day. The lady is wearing a blouse, a wrapper and matching head gear. Sometimes a shawl called an "iborun" is either tied around the waist or hung loosely on the shoulder. The man is wearing a long flowing robe (called an agbada) over a kaftan and a pair of pants (trousers) with a cap to match.

The Fulanis

Fulani is mainly spoken in the northern part of Nigeria, in Sokoto, Katsina, Kano and Kaduna states.

The Fulanis unified the Hausa states by launching a Jihad (holy war), led by Usman Dan Fodio in the 19th century. The traditional Fulani occupation is cattle rearing. They are nomadic people and move from place to place to find food and water for their cattle.

Traditional Fulani food crops include corn, millet, sorghum, cassava, sugarcane and nuts. A popular Fulani meal is a porridge (made with sorghum, millet or corn) and eaten with a soup made with vegetables, tomatoes and various spices.

Fulani Proverbs:

Nobody is without knowledge except those who ask no questions.

It is not only the fox; even the snail arrives at his destination.

Lady in a short blouse and a wrapper, traditionally worn by Fulani milk maids.

The Ijaws

Ijaw is mainly spoken in the Niger-Delta, in Bayelsa, Delta and Rivers states. Ijaw is also spoken in some parts of Akwa-Ibom, Edo and Ondo states.

Like the Igbos, many Ijaws traditionally lived in separate local societies and villages and were not governed by a single governing body.

The major traditional occupations of the Ijaws are fishing and farming. The Ijaws live in the Niger-Delta, and thus are surrounded by water, which has fueled their fishing occupation.

Typical Ijaw food crops include yams, cocoyams, plantains and bananas. A common Ijaw meal is Kekefiyai (a mixture of chopped plantains, vegetables, fish and various spices).

Ijaw Proverbs:

The crocodile says he is shy to bite, but when he bites, he is shy to let go.

The frog says it likes water, but not when it is boiling.

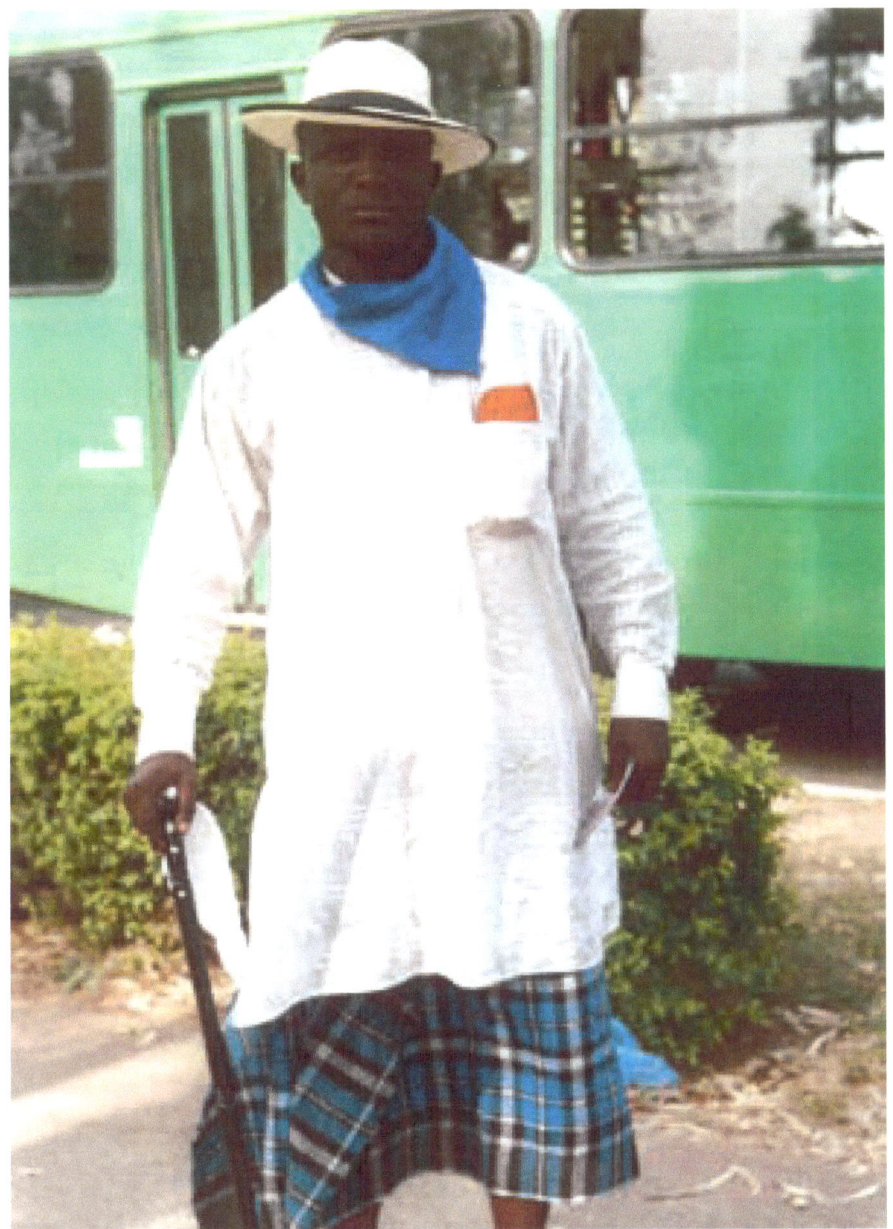

A man in modern traditional Ijaw dressing: a long flowing shirt or blouse, a wrapper bundled at the waist and a matching cap.

The Kanuris

Borno state is the main state occupied by the Kanuris in Nigeria. Borno is located in the northeastern part of Nigeria.

The Kanuris of Nigeria were originally a part of the ancient Kanem-Bornu Empire.

The Kanuris traditionally engage in farming and their most important food crop is millet. The Kanuris also traditionally engage in some fishing, especially in Lake Chad. Lake Chad borders Nigeria on the northeast.

A common Kanuri food is millet made into porridge and served with soup made with tomatoes, peppers and various spices.

Kanuri Proverbs:

Hold a true friend with both hands.

One does not love if one cannot accept from others.

A man in modern traditional Kanuri dressing, which consists of a long kaftan (usually embroidered in the middle) and a pair of pants (trousers) with a matching cap.

The Ibibios

Ibibio is mainly spoken in what is called the south-south (or the deep south) part of Nigeria, in Akwa Ibom state.

The Ibibios are said to have lived in the areas they currently occupy since before the 1800s.

The traditional occupation of the Ibibios is farming, and they grow food crops that include yams, cassava, coco-yams, plantains and pumpkins. Another major occupation of the Ibibios is fishing. Historically, the main food crop of the Ibibios is the Palm tree, from which palm oil is extracted for family sustenance and for sale to neighboring villages.

A popular Ibibio meal is edikainkong (a soup made with chopped pumpkin leaves and different types of meat) served with a starch like pounded yam (looks like mashed potatoes but thicker).

Ibibio Proverbs:

A lion gave birth to you, yet you are acting like a goat.

A man that falls uses the ground as support to stand up.

A woman in modern traditional Ibibio dressing, which like the Igbos, consists of a beautiful blouse, two wrappers (one long and one short) and a matching head gear.

The Tivs

The Tiv language is mainly spoken in the northern part of Nigeria, in Benue, Taraba and Nasarawa states.

The Tivs are said to be descendants of a man named Tiv.

The traditional occupation of the Tivs is farming, and they grow food crops such as cassavas, sweet potatoes, yams, peanuts, sorghum, millet and maize.

A popular Tiv meal consists of slices of "sweet yams" boiled or fried and eaten with a sauce made with tomatoes and various spices.

Tiv Proverbs:

A horse often falls even though it has four legs.

The hippo blocked the road and nobody could get across.

Tiv dancers at a cultural festival in Nigeria. The Tivs are known for their striped white and black traditional clothing.

THE GOVERNMENT

Nigeria operates a presidential system of government, which consists of a national federal government and thirty-six state governments.

The national federal government is divided into three branches: the executive branch (led by the President), the legislative branch (the National Assembly) and the judicial branch (led by the Supreme Court).

The President is in charge of supervising the executive branch as it executes or enforces the laws of the country. The President of Nigeria is the Head of State, the Head of Government and the Commander in Chief of the Nigerian Armed Forces. The President of Nigeria is elected by direct popular vote of the citizens of the country to a four-year term. The President may serve two four-year terms if he or she is reelected for a second term.

To be eligible for election to the Presidency, an individual must be at least forty years old, a citizen of Nigeria, have completed at least his or her Secondary School (High School) education and must be sponsored by a political party. The Presidential house is called Aso Rock (named after a rock in Abuja).

The National Assembly is the supreme law making body of Nigeria. The National Assembly is divided into the Senate and the House Representatives, just like in the United States of America. The Senate is referred to as the Upper Chamber. The Senate is led by the President of the Senate and has 109 members. The members of the senate are voted into the senate by direct election of the citizens of their respective states. Each of the thirty-six state elects three senators to represent its state in the Senate and the Federal Capital Territory, Abuja, elects one senator to the Senate.

On the other hand, the House of Representatives is referred to as the Lower Chamber. The House of Representatives is led by the Speaker of the House and has 360 members elected by direct popular election of the citizens of Nigeria.

To be eligible for election to the Senate, an individual must be at least thirty-five years old, a citizen of Nigeria, have completed at least his or her Secondary School (High School) education and must be sponsored by a political party. To be eligible for election to the House, on the other hand, an individual must be at least thirty years old, a citizen of Nigeria, have completed at least his or her Secondary School (High School) education and must be sponsored by a political party.

The National Assembly building in Abuja.

The Supreme Court of Nigeria.

The Supreme Court of Nigeria is the head body in charge of interpreting the laws of the land.

The Court is headed by the Chief Justice of the Supreme Court and assisted by other co-justices not to exceed twenty-one justices as provided by the Constitution of the Federal Republic of Nigeria.

The President of Nigeria nominates justices to the Supreme Court on the recommendation of the National Judicial Council and such Justices as are nominated are then appointed after confirmation by the Senate.

To be eligible for appointment to the Court, an individual must have been qualified to practice as a legal practitioner in Nigeria for at least the previous fifteen years before the nomination.

Aso Rock, the National Assembly and the Supreme Court buildings are located in Abuja in close proximity to one another in what is known as the Three Arms Zone or TAZ.

Heads of State
1960 to 2012

Alhaji Sir Abubakar Tafawa Balewa

Prime Minister
1960 – 1966

Alhaji Sir Tafawa Balewa served as the first Prime Minister of Nigeria after the country gained independence. His leadership lasted from 1960 to 1966. Born in Tafawa Balewa, Bauchi State, he became the Prime Minister on Independence Day, October 1, 1960, and held the position until January 15, 1966. During his reign as Prime Minister, Nigeria also had a president called Dr. Nnamdi Azikiwe.

Tafawa Balewa appears on the 5 Naira note. Nigeria's currency is made up of Naira notes and Kobo coins.

Dr. Benjamin Nnamdi Azikiwe

First President (First Head of State)
1963 – 1966

Dr. Nnamdi Azikiwe was the first President of the Federal Republic of Nigeria. He is the only President to serve as a ceremonial President of Nigeria. Azikiwe held the position from October 1, 1963 to January 16, 1966. He was the President of Nigeria during the time that Tafawa Balewa was the Prime Minister. Azikiwe was overthrown from his presidential position during a military coup.

Azikiwe appears on the 500 Naira note. Nigeria's currency is made up of Naira notes and Kobo coins. He was popularly known as "Zik" or the "Great Zik of Africa." He was known for saying "Talk, I listen. You listen, I talk."

Major General Johnson Thomas Umunnakwe Aguiyi Ironsi

First Military Head of State (Second Head of State)

1966

Major General Aguiyi Ironsi was the first military Head of State and Commander in Chief of the Armed Forces. He came to power through a military coup on January 16, 1966, and was overthrown during a military coup on July 29, 1966. His regime lasted for about seven months.

General Yakubu Gowon
Second Military Head of State (Third Head of State)
1966 – 1975

General Yakubu Gowon was the Head of State from August 1, 1966 to July 29, 1975. During the Nigerian civil war that lasted for about 3 years, many groups in the south – notably the Igbos – sought to separate from Nigeria and create a separate country, which was to be called the Republic of Biafra.

Gowon's government prevented the Biafran separation from Nigeria. The war began in July of 1967, and officially ended in January of 1970.

Biafra gets its name from a coastal area in Africa, located around the Gulf of Guinea, which was called the Bight of

Biafra at the time of the war, but is now known as the Bight of Bonny.

Gowon came to power through a military coup in 1966 and was removed from power during a military coup in 1975.

General Murtala Ramat Mohammed

Third Military Head of State (Fourth Head of State)
1975 – 1976

General Murtala Mohammed became Head of State after the military coup that removed General Yakubu Gowon from power. General Mohammed was the Head of State for about six months from July 29, 1975 to February 13, 1976. He was named Head of State and Commander in Chief of the Armed Forces on July 29, 1975, following a military coup. He was assassinated on February 13, 1976 during an unsuccessful coup. He is on the 20 Naira note. Nigeria's currency is made up of Naira notes and Kobo coins.

General Olusegun Obasanjo
Fourth Military Head of State (Fifth Head of State)
1976 – 1979

General Obasanjo became the Head of State on February 13, 1976, after the assassination of General Murtala Mohammed in an abortive coup. On October 1, 1979, he became the first military leader in Africa to willingly hand over power to a civilian government. He also became a democratically elected president in 1999. He is the only person who has served as Nigeria's Head of State more than once.

Alhaji Shehu Usman Aliyu Shagari

Second President (Sixth Head of State)
1979 – 1983

Alhaji Shehu Shagari was the first democratically elected executive president of Nigeria. Shagari's government lasted from October 1, 1979 to December 31, 1983. His government was ousted by a military coup led by Major General Muhammadu Buhari on New Year's Eve in 1983.

Major General Muhammadu Buhari

Fifth Military Head of State (Seventh Head of State)
1984 – 1985

Major General Buhari became the Head of State on January 1, 1984, after a military coup that removed Alhaji Shagari from the presidency. Buhari's government ended on August 27, 1985, when his government was overthrown from power by a military coup led by General Ibrahim Babaginda.

General Ibrahim Badamosi Babangida

Sixth Military Head of State (Eighth Head of State)
1985 – 1993

General Ibrahim Babaginda was the Head of State and Commander in Chief of the Armed Forces from 1985 to 1993. Popularly known by his initials, IBB, he came into power on August 27, 1985 by overthrowing the government of Major Buhari. On August 26, 1993, he handed over power to Chief Shonekan, who was supposed to administer Nigeria's transition into a democratic government.

Chief Ernest Adegunle Oladeinde Shonekan

Third President (Ninth Head of State)
1993

On August 26, 1993, General Babangida appointed Chief Shonekan as the interim president and head of the transitional government. Shonekan's government lasted for only three months before it was overthrown by General Abacha on November 17, 1993.

General Sani Abacha

Seventh Military Head of State (Tenth Head of State)
1993 – 1998

General Abacha was the Head of State from November 17, 1993 to June 8, 1998. General Abacha obtained the position by seizing power from the transitional government of Chief Shonekan. General Abacha's government ended abruptly upon his death in June of 1998.

General Abdullsalami Abubakar

Eighth Military Head of State (Eleventh Head of State)
1998 – 1999

General Abubakar was appointed the military Head of State after General Abacha's death. General Abubakar's government lasted from June 8, 1998 to May 29, 1999, when he handed over power to a democratically elected president. His government is noted for returning Nigeria to democracy.

Chief Olusegun Obasanjo

Fourth President (Twelfth Head of State)
1999 – 2007

Chief Obasanjo became the Head of State of Nigeria for the second time on May 29, 1999. He had previously held the position of Head of State from 1976 to 1979. In 1979, he became the first African military leader to willingly hand over power to a civilian government. His second government ended in May 2007 after completing two four-year terms.

Alhaji Umaru Musa Yar'Adua

Fifth President (Thirteenth Head of State)
2007 to 2010

On May 29, 2007, Alhaji Yar'Adua became the president of Nigeria after Chief Obasanjo's second term. It was the first time in the country's history that a civilian government handed power to another civilian government, and the third time that any President or Head of State of Nigeria handed over power willingly to another government. The first time was when the same Chief Obasanjo's government willingly transferred power to a civilian government in 1979. Yar'Adua's presidency ended upon his death after a long illness. He died on May 5, 2010.

Mr. Goodluck Ebele Azikiwe Jonathan

Fifth President (Fourteenth Head of State)
2011 – Present

On May 6, 2010, Mr. Goodluck Jonathan was appointed president of Nigeria. Prior to becoming president, Mr. Jonathan served as the vice-president of Nigeria during President Yar'Adua's presidency. He was appointed to act as president during Yar'Adua's long illness, and then sworn in as President of Nigeria on May 6, 2010, the day following Yar'Adua's death on May 5, 2010. Presidential elections were held the following year. Jonathan won the presidential elections and his inauguration was on May 29, 2011.

The National Anthem

Arise O compatriots,
Nigeria's call obey
To serve our fatherland
With love and strength and faith
The labor of our heroes past
Shall never be in vain
To serve with heart and might
One nation bound in freedom,
Peace and unity.

Oh God of creation,
Direct our noble cause
Guide our leaders right
Help our youths the truth to know
In love and honesty to grow
And living just and true
Great lofty heights attain
To build a nation where peace
And justice shall reign.

The National Anthem was adopted on October 1, 1978. This anthem replaced the previous anthem, *Nigeria, We Hail Thee,* which was adopted in 1960 and written by a British expatriate. Benedict E. Odiase, who was the Director of Music for the Nigerian Police Band, composed the music for the current National Anthem.

The National Pledge

I pledge to Nigeria my country
To be faithful, loyal and honest
To serve Nigeria with all my strength
To defend her unity
And uphold her honor and glory
So help me God.

Pupils of Model Primary School, Gwarinpa, Abuja, reciting the National Pledge.

National Holidays - Nigeria

National Holidays	Dates
New Year's Day	January 1
Id el Fitr	As Declared
Id el Kabir	As Declared
Good Friday	March/April (As Declared)
Easter Monday	March/April (As Declared)
Workers' Day	May 1
Children's Day	May 27
Democracy Day	May 29
Independence Day	October 1
Id el Maulud	As Declared
Christmas Day	December 25
Boxing Day	December 26

Holidays labeled "As Declared" are religious holidays and the dates on which they are observed vary from year to year. Each year, the proper authorities confirm the dates for observance of those religious holidays.

States of Nigeria	Capital Cities
Abia	Umuahia
Adamawa	Yola
Akwa Ibom	Uyo
Anambra	Awka
Bauchi	Bauchi
Bayelsa	Yenogoa
Benue	Makurdi
Borno	Maiduguri
Cross River	Calabar
Delta	Asaba
Ebonyi	Abakaliki
Ekiti	Ado-Ekiti
Edo	Benin
Enugu	Enugu
Gombe	Gombe
Imo	Owerri
Jigawa	Dutse
Kaduna	Kaduna
Kano	Kano
Katsina	Katsina
Kebbi	Birnin Kebbi
Kogi	Lokoja
Kwara	Ilorin
Lagos	Ikeja
Nasarawa	Lafia
Niger	Minna
Ogun	Abeokuta
Ondo	Akure
Osun	Osogbo
Oyo	Ibadan
Plateau	Jos
Rivers	Port Harcourt
Sokoto	Sokoto
Taraba	Jalingo
Yobe	Damaturu
Zamfara	Gusau

Test Yourself

1. What is the name of the river after which Nigeria is named? Page 6

2. What do the colors of the Nigerian flag represent? Page 14

3. What is the national flower of Nigeria? Page 8

4. What is the date of Nigeria's independence? Page 58

5. What is the date of the national holiday reserved for celebrating children? Page 58

6. What are the names of the three largest ethnic groups in Nigeria? Page 17

7. How many states are in Nigeria? Page 11

8. What is the name of the federal capital territory of Nigeria? Page 15

9. What state is the economic center of Nigeria? Page 16

10. What system of government does Nigerian have? Page 34

11. What date is Democracy day? Page 58

12. What is the name of this Book?

13. What is the official language spoken in Nigeria? Page 17

14. What is the name of the first president of Nigeria? Page 41

15. Write or recite the National Pledge? Page 57

16. In the National Anthem, what do we ask God to help the youths to know? Page 56

17. What are the names of the countries that are Nigeria's neighbors on the east side? Page 6

18. What are the names of the two seasons in Nigeria? Page 12

19. The name Nigeria is a combination of two words. What are they? Page 6

Sources and For More Information:

www.absoluteastronomy.com

www.brittanica.com

www.cenbank.org/currency/issuessys.asp

www.cia.gov/library/publications/the-world-factbook/geos.NI.html

www.flagspot.net

Helen Chapin Metz, ed. Nigeria: A Country Study. Washington: GPO for the Library of Congress, 1991

www.mapsofworld.com

www.motherlandnigeria.org

www.nassnig.org

www.nigerianembassyusa.org

www.nigeria-consulate-atl.org

The Constitution of the Federal Republic of Nigeria (see www.nigeria-law.org, for online version of the Constitution)

www.waado.org

www.theworldtravelguide.net